The Thinker's Guide to

TAKING CHARGE OF THE HUMAN MIND

Thinking, Feeling, Wanting, and The Problem of Irrationality

FOURTH EDITION, REVISED AND EXPANDED

LINDA ELDER and RICHARD PAUL

ROWMAN & LITTLEFIELD
Lanham • Boulder • New York • London

Originally published by
The Foundation for Critical Thinking
1-800-833-3645
www.criticalthinking.org

Reissued in 2019 by Rowman & Littlefield
An imprint of The Rowman & Littlefield Publishing Group, Inc.
4501 Forbes Boulevard, Suite 200, Lanham, Maryland 20706
www.rowman.com

6 Tinworth Street, London SE11 5AL, United Kingdom

British Library Cataloguing in Publication Information Available

Library of Congress Cataloging-in-Publication Data

Elder, Linda
The thinker's guide to taking charge of the human mind: thinking, feeling, wanting, and the problem of irrationality
Linda Elder, Richard Paul
ISBN 978-0-944583-58-6 (pbk: alk. paper) | ISBN 978-1-5381-3388-0 (electronic)
1. theory of mind 2. irrationality 3. egocentricity 4. sociocentricity 5. cognition and affect 6. thinking and emotions 7. critical thinking and emotions 8. ethnocentricity
2013957774

∞™ The paper used in this publication meets the minimum requirements of American National Standard for Information Sciences—Permanence of Paper for Printed Library Materials, ANSI/NISO Z39.48-1992.

The Foundation for Critical Thinking and the Thinker's Guide Library

Founded by Dr. Richard Paul, the Foundation for Critical Thinking is the longest-running non-profit organization dedicated to critical thinking. Through seminars and conferences, online courses and resources, and a wide range of publications, the Foundation promotes critical societies by cultivating essential intellectual abilities and virtues in every field of study and professional area. Learn more at www.criticalthinking.org and visit the Center for Critical Thinking Community Online (criticalthinkingcommunity.org).

The Thinker's Guide Library introduces the Paul-Elder Framework for Critical Thinking™ and contextualizes critical thinking across subject areas and audience levels to foster fair-minded critical reasoning throughout the world.

1. The Miniature Guide to Critical Thinking Concepts & Tools, Eighth Edition
2. The Thinker's Guide to Analytic Thinking
3. The Thinker's Guide to Ethical Reasoning
4. The Thinker's Guide to Socratic Questioning
5. The Thinker's Guide to Fallacies
6. The Nature and Functions of Critical & Creative Thinking
7. The Art of Asking Essential Questions, Fifth Edition
8. The Thinker's Guide to the Human Mind
9. The Thinker's Guide for Conscientious Citizens on How to Detect Media Bias and Propaganda in National and World News, Fourth Edition
10. The Thinker's Guide to Scientific Thinking
11. The Thinker's Guide to Engineering Reasoning
12. The Thinker's Guide to Clinical Reasoning
13. The Aspiring Thinker's Guide to Critical Thinking
14. The Student Guide to Historical Thinking
15. The Thinker's Guide for Students on How to Study & Learn a Discipline, Second Edition
16. How to Read a Paragraph: The Art of Close Reading, Second Edition
17. How to Write a Paragraph: The Art of Substantive Writing
18. The International Critical Thinking Reading and Writing Test, Second Edition
19. The Miniature Guide to Practical Ways for Promoting Active and Cooperative Learning, Third Edition
20. How to Improve Student Learning: 30 Practical Ideas
21. A Critical Thinker's Guide to Educational Fads
22. The Thinker's Guide to Intellectual Standards
23. A Guide for Educators to Critical Thinking Competency Standards

Foreword

To live well is to live as a reasonable and ethical person.

Yet humans are not by nature rational or ethical. Humans are predisposed to operate in the world in narrow terms of how it can serve them. Their brains are directly wired into their own pleasure and pain, not that of others. They do not automatically consider the rights and needs of others.

However, humans have the raw capacity to become reasonable and ethical persons, to develop as fairminded skilled thinkers. But to do so requires:

1. Understanding how the mind works.
2. Using this understanding to develop skills and insights.

This guide addresses the first of these requirements. It lays the conceptual foundations necessary for understanding the mind, its functions, its natural propensity toward irrationality, and its capacity for rationality.

It is designed for those interested in developing their potential to be fairminded reasonable persons, concerned with how their behavior affects the lives of others, concerned to develop their full humanity, concerned with making the world a more civilized and just place.

It is designed for those willing to transform their thinking to improve their decisions, the quality of their lives, the quality of their interpersonal relationships, and their vision of the world.

It is intended to provide an initial map to help interested persons begin to free themselves from the traps their minds have constructed. It begins to detail the intrinsic egocentric and sociocentric tendencies that give rise to irrationality in human life and human thought. It points the way toward mindfulness and self-understanding through critical thinking.

Contents

As humans we live in our **Minds**

Understanding The Human Mind: The Big Picture

The mind is its own place
and in itself
can make a hell of heaven
or a heaven of hell
– John Milton

Everyone thinks. It is our nature to do so. But much of our thinking left to itself is biased, distorted, ill-founded, or prejudiced. Much of our thinking leads to problems in our lives. Much of our thinking leads to cruelty and injustice. Of course, the mind doesn't just think, it also feels and wants. What is the connection?

Our thinking shapes and determines how we feel and what we want. When we think well, we are motivated to do things that make sense and motivated to act in ways that help rather than harm ourselves and others.

At the same time, powerful emotions or desires influence our thinking, help or hinder how well we think in a situation. At any given moment, our minds (that complex of inner thoughts, feelings and desires) can be under the sway of our native irrationality or our potential reasonability. When we are ruled by our irrational tendencies, we see the world from a narrow self-serving perspective. We are not truly concerned with how our behavior affects others. We are fundamentally concerned with getting what we want and/or with validating our beliefs and views.

The key to understanding human thought then, is, to understand its essential duality: its capacity for irrationality (being trapped in egocentric and/or sociocentric thought with its attendant self-deception, self-delusion, rationalization, and so forth)) and its capacity for reasonability (freeing itself from self-delusion, myth, and illusion).

Though thinking, feeling and wanting are, in principle, equally important, it is only through thinking that we take command of our minds. It is through thinking that we figure out what is going wrong with our thinking. It is through thinking that we figure out how to deal with destructive emotions. It is through thinking that we change unproductive desires to productive ones. It is fairminded reasonability that frees us from intellectual slavery and conformity.

If we understand our mind and its functions, if we face the barriers to our development caused by egocentric and sociocentric thought, if we work upon our mind in a daily regimen, we can take the steps that lead to our empowerment as thinkers.

The Mind's Three Distinctive Functions

The mind has three basic functions: thinking, feeling, and wanting.

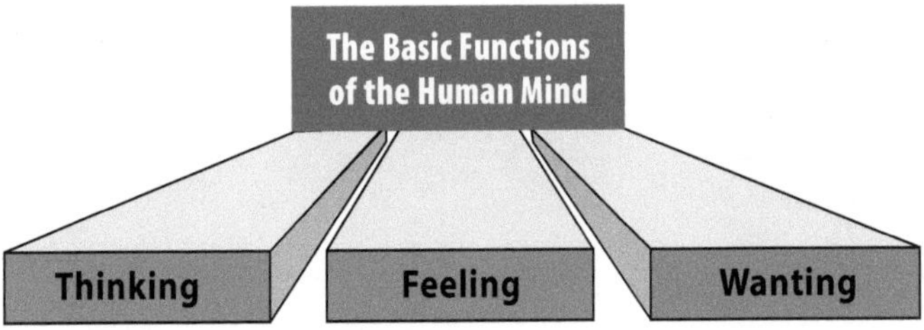

- Thinking is the part of the mind that figures things out. It makes sense of life's events. It creates the ideas through which we define situations, relationships and problems. It continually tells us: This is what is going on. This is what is happening. Notice this and that.
- Feelings[1*] are created by thinking — evaluating whether the events of our lives are positive or negative. Feelings continually tell us: "This is how I should feel about what is happening in my life. I'm doing really well." Or, alternatively, "Things aren't going well for me."
- Our desires allocate energy to action, in keeping with what we define as desirable and possible. It continually tells us: "This is worth getting. Go for it!" Or, conversely, "This is not worth getting. Don't bother."

* When we speak of feelings, we are not referring to emotions caused by dysfunctional biological processes such as problems in brain chemistry. When emotions are caused by imbalances in brain chemistry which people cannot control themselves, clinical help may be needed. When we speak of feelings, we are also not referring to bodily sensations, though feelings often accompany bodily sensations. For instance being "cold" might cause you to feel irritable. Recognizing the feeling of irritability might lead you to something about being cold, like putting on a jacket. Finally, though the terms "feelings" and "emotions" might be used in some cases to refer to different phenomena, we use these terms interchangeably in this guide.

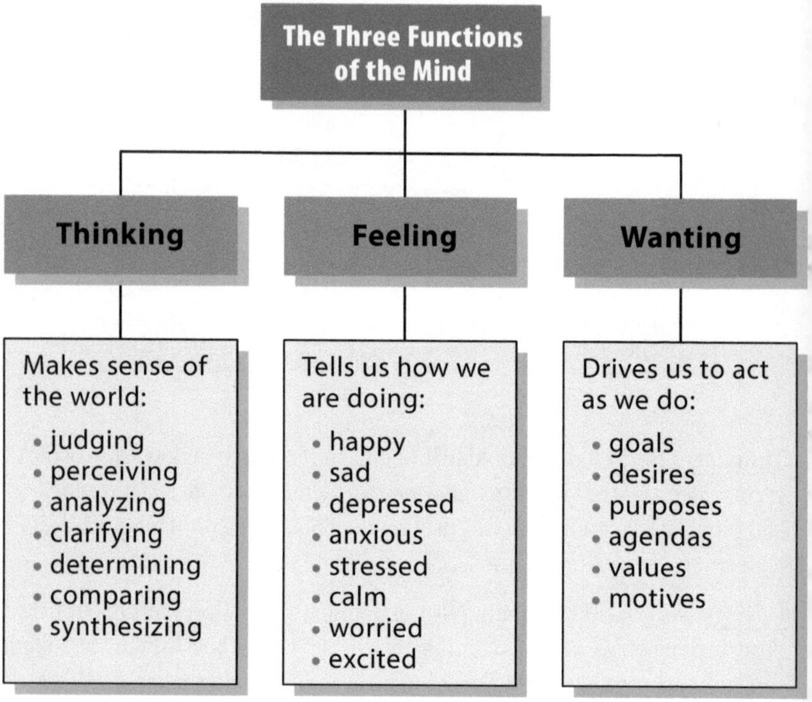

Essential Idea: Our mind is continually communicating three kinds of things to us:

1) what is going on in life,
2) feelings (positive or negative) about those events, and
3) things to pursue, where to put our energy (in light of 1 and 2).

The Dynamic Relationship Between Thinking, Feeling, Wanting

There is an intimate, dynamic interrelation between thinking, feeling, and wanting. Each is continually influencing the other two.

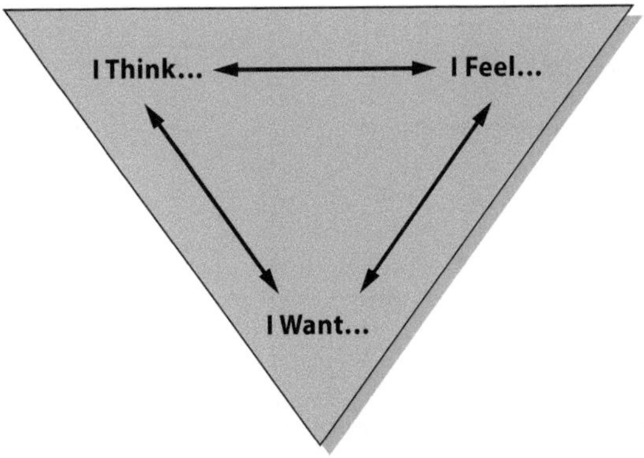

For example, when we think we are being threatened, we feel fear, and we inevitably want to flee from or attack whatever we think is threatening us. When we feel depressed, we think that there is nothing we can do to improve our situation, and we therefore lack the motivation to do anything about our situation. When we want to improve our eating habits it may be because we think that our diet is causing us harm and we feel dissatisfied with our diet.

Though we can consider the functions of the mind separately (to better understand them), they can never be absolutely separated. Imagine them as a triangle with three necessary sides: thoughts, feelings and desires. Eliminate one side of the triangle and it collapses. Each side depends on the other two. In other words, without thinking there can be no feelings or desires; without feelings, no thoughts or desires; without desires, no thoughts or feelings. For example, it is unintelligible to imagine thinking that something is threatening you and might harm you, wanting to escape from it, yet feeling nothing in relationship to what you think and want. Because you think you might be harmed and you want to flee, you necessarily feel fear.

Behavior: A Product of the Mind's Functions

Thoughts, feelings and desires continually interact, and produce behavior as a result of that interaction. To understand this, consider the example on the previous page about eating habits. Suppose you feel dissatisfied with your diet. You want to improve your diet because you think that by doing so you will improve your health.

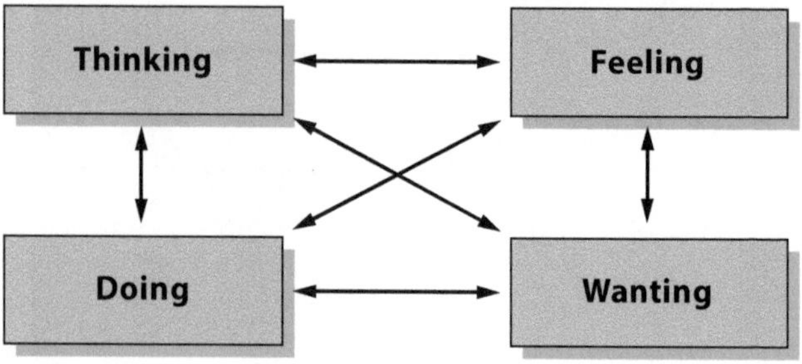

You therefore behave in the following ways:

1. read about different diets (behavior),
2. come to conclusions about the best diet for you, then change your diet accordingly.

After a few weeks you notice that you feel better physically and are losing weight. You now feel satisfied. You think that your diet is improving your health. You therefore want to continue with the new diet.

But then after a few more weeks you think: "I don't want to eat any more salads and tasteless foods. I can't keep this up for the rest of my life! There must be a diet available that is not boring." You therefore act on that thinking. Again you consider different diet possibilities, finally deciding upon a new diet. The process begins again, with thoughts, feelings, desires, continually shaping behavior.

Thinking as the Key to Feelings and Desires

Though thoughts, feelings and desires play equally important roles in the mind, continually influencing and being influenced by one another, thinking is the key to command of feelings and desires. To change a feeling is to change the thinking that leads to the feeling. To change a desire is to change the thinking that underlies the desire.

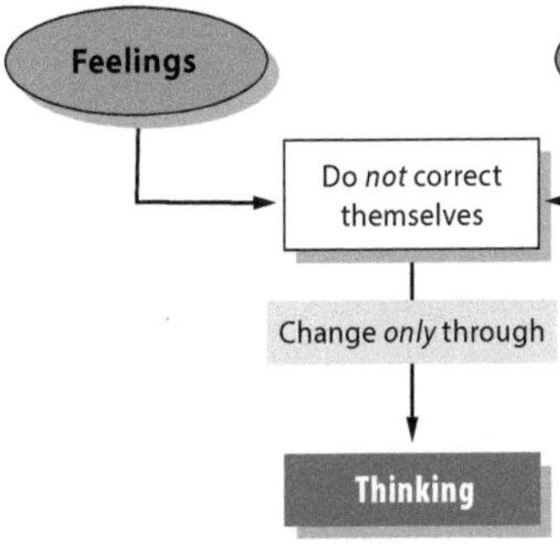

If I feel angry because my child is behaving disrespectfully toward me, I can't simply replace anger with satisfaction, for example. To change the anger to a more positive emotion, I must change the thinking I am doing in the situation. Perhaps I need to think about how to teach my child to behave respectfully towards me, and then behave in accordance with that new thinking. Perhaps I need to think about the influences in my child's life that might be causing the rude behavior and then try to eliminate those influences. In other words, I get control of my emotional state through my thinking.

Similarly we can't change a desire without changing the thinking that causes the desire. Suppose, for example, two people, Jan and John, have been in a romantic relationship but John has broken off the relationship. Yet Jan still wants to be in the relationship. Suppose that her desire comes from thinking (that may be unconscious) that she needs to be in the relationship to be emotionally stable, that she won't be able to function without John. Clearly this thinking is the problem. Jan must therefore change her thinking so she no longer wants a relationship with John. In other words, until she thinks that she does not need John to be OK, that she can function satisfactorily without him, that she doesn't need to be in a relationship with a person who doesn't want to be with her, she will want to be in the relationship with John. In short, unless her thinking changes, her desire won't change. She must defeat the thinking that is defeating her.

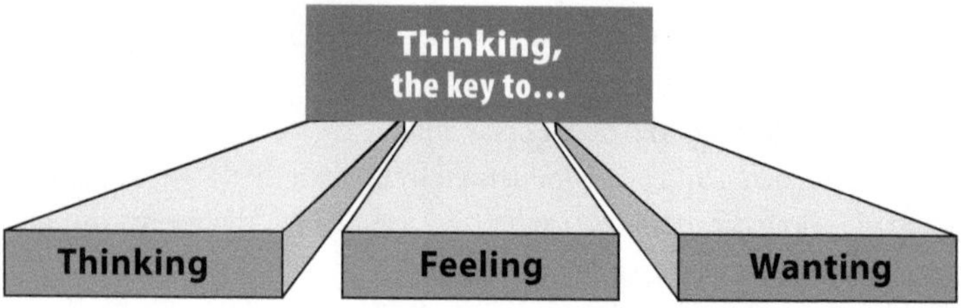
Thinking,
the key to...
Thinking
Feeling
Wanting

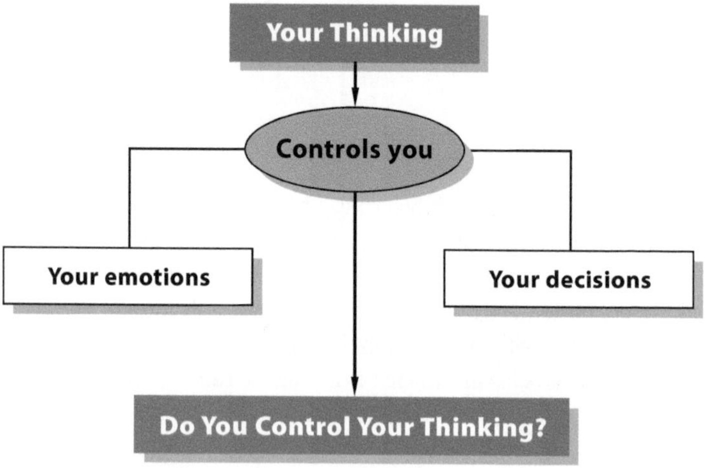
Your Thinking
Controls you
Your emotions
Your decisions
Do You Control Your Thinking?

Rational Capacities or Irrational Tendencies Can Control the Mind

The three functions of the mind — thoughts, feelings and desires — can be guided or directed either by one's native irrationality or by one's rational capacities.
Irrational tendencies function automatically and largely unconsciously. Rational tendencies tend to arise from active self-development and are largely conscious.
Irrationality can be principally categorized according to whether and to what degree it is egocentric and/or sociocentric in nature. Egocentric thought, as we refer to it in this guide, is focused on the pursuit of one's own desires and needs without regard to the rights and needs of others. Sociocentric thought is focused on the pursuit of group goals without regard to the rights and needs of those outside the group. Detailing and unpacking the concepts of egocentric and sociocentric thought, in juxtaposition with rationality or reasonability, are the primary emphasis of the rest of the guide.

Egocentricity

Egocentricity exists in two forms: skilled and unskilled. Both pursue selfish ends. Highly skilled egocentric persons use their intelligence to effectively rationalize gaining their selfish ends at the expense of others. They skillfully distort information to serve their interest. They are often articulate in arguing for their ends (which they typically cover with altruistic language). They hide their prejudices well. Naïve others often fail to see their selfish core (masked, as it is, in an ethical or seemingly considerate façade). They often succeed in moving up the social ladder and gain prestigious jobs and honored positions. Skilled egocentric persons may favor either domination or submission, but often combine both in effective ways. For example, they may successfully dominate persons "below" them while they are subtly servile to those "above" them. They know how to tell people what they want to hear. They are consummate manipulators and often hold positions of power.

Unskilled egocentric persons are unsuccessful in pursuing their selfish ends because many see through them and do not trust them. Their prejudices and narrowness are more obvious and less schooled. They often have blatantly dysfunctional relationships with others. They are often trapped in negative emotions they do not understand. Unskilled egocentric persons may prefer either domination or submission as a means of getting what they want, but whichever they use, they are usually unsuccessful at either. Sometimes they are overtly cruel or play the victim in openly self-pitying ways.

Sociocentricity

As humans, we are all born centered in ourselves. As part of our native egocentricity, we feel directly and unavoidably our own pain and frustration, our own joy and pleasure.
We largely see the world from a narrow, self-serving perspective. But we humans are also

social animals. We must interact with others to survive as beings in the world. In interacting with others in groups we form complex belief systems. These belief systems often reflect a variety of forms of intellectual blindness as well as intellectual insights. In living a human life, we develop world views that are a mixture of self-serving, group- serving, and rational thought.

Our social groups not only provide us with ways and means of surviving; they also impose on us relatively narrow ways of looking at the world. And they powerfully influence our thoughts and actions. Our intrinsic narrowness of perspective, focused on our own needs and wants, merges with our group views as we are increasingly socialized and conditioned, over time, to see the world, not only from our own point of view but from the perspective of our groups: family, gender, peers, colleagues, ethnic group, nationality, religion, profession, and so forth.

Sociocentric thought is the native human tendency to see the world from narrow and biased group-centered perspectives, to operate within the world through group rules, group interests. It is intimately connected with the human "need" for validation — the innate need to be accepted and esteemed by others.

Rationality

Rationality is properly thought of as a way of thinking and acting in which intelligence and sound reasoning are used to serve justice, in which the actor adheres to the same standards by which he judges his enemy, in which he does not need to rationalize or project a false façade to impress others. Successful powerful people are often intelligent, unreasonable, and unscrupulous—all in one. They often cannot openly admit the games they play to obtain social and economic success. They often suppress evidence that puts them in a bad light. Reasonable people, on the other hand, respect the rights and needs of others, are flexible, open-minded, and just. They have intellectual integrity as well as intellectual humility and perseverance. They have confidence in reason and follow its lead. They are able to enter empathically into the point of view of others. They do not misuse language. They say what they mean and mean what they say.

Rationality is sometimes wrongly thought of as covering both those who intelligently and successfully pursue selfish ends and those who intelligently and successfully pursue unselfish ends. We believe that those who intelligently pursue selfish ends are those described below as skilled egocentric persons. In other words, we do not think that those who sophistically manipulate people to act against their interests and consequently lack integrity, are properly called "reasonable" persons. Consummate manipulators, however skilled and successful, are not reasonable persons (since they would be the first to object to being treated as they routinely treat others).

The Human Mind is Frequently Irrational While Having the Capacity for Rational Thought

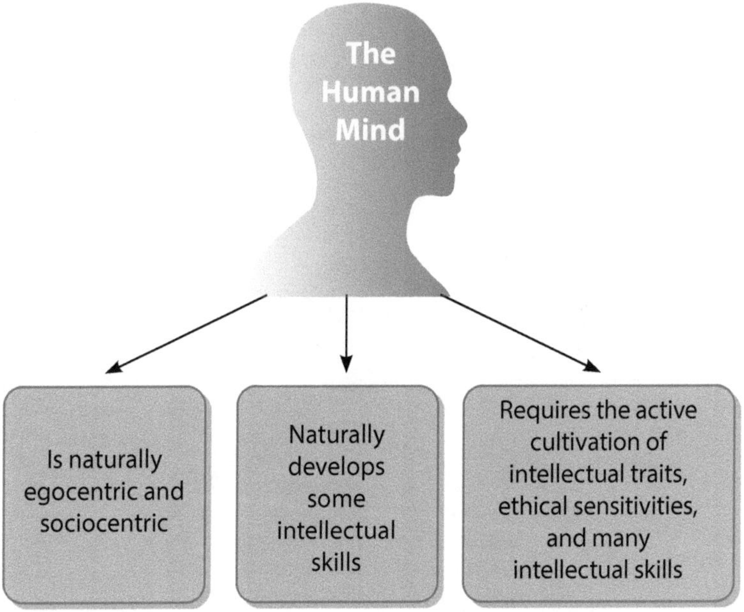

Essential Idea: All humans are innately egocentric and sociocentric. Humans also have (largely undeveloped) rational capacities. Humans begin life as primarily egocentric creatures. Over time, infantile egocentric self-centered thinking merges with sociocentric group-centered thinking. All humans regularly engage in both forms of irrational thought. The extent to which any of us is egocentric or sociocentric is a matter of degree and can change significantly in various situations or contexts. While egocentric and sociocentric propensities are naturally occurring phenomena, rational capacities must be largely developed. It is through the development of rational capacities that we combat irrational tendencies and cultivate critical societies.

The Logic of Rationality

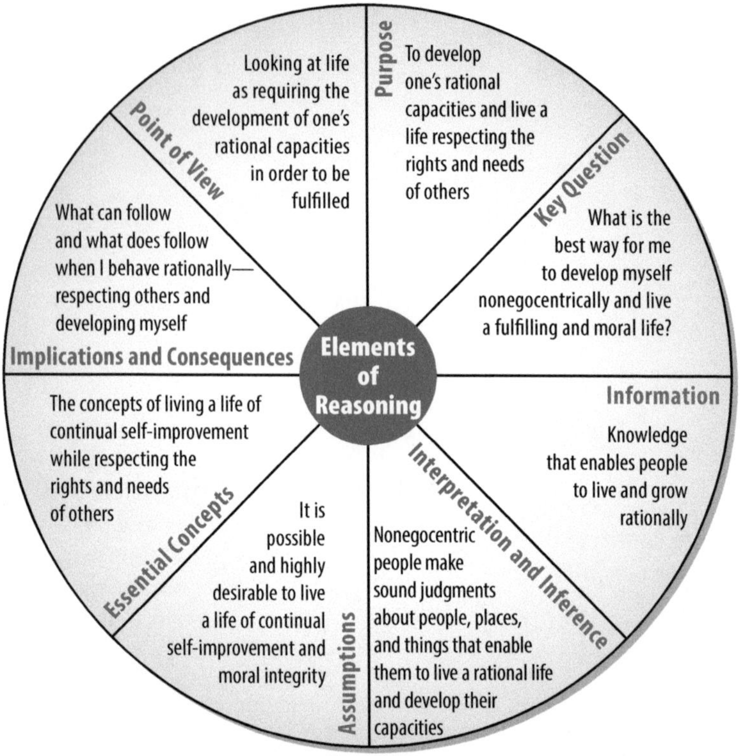

Distinguishing Rational from Egocentric and Sociocentric Motives

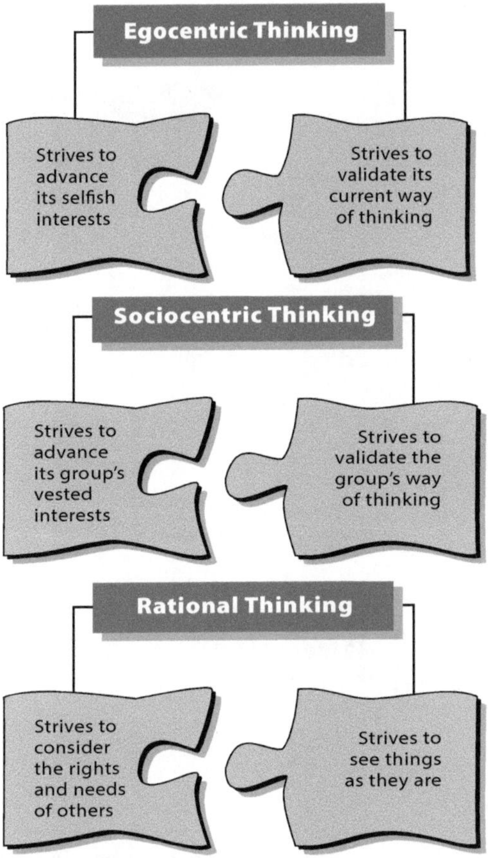

Essential Idea: Though egocentric, sociocentric and rational thought may be complex, we can capture their basic motives.

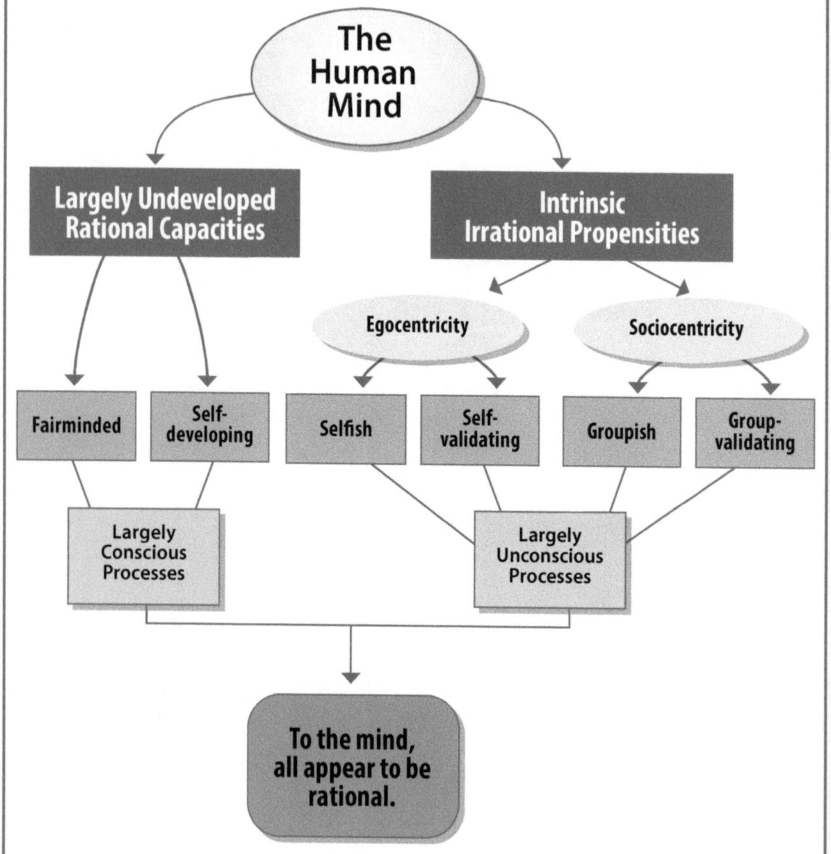

Essential Idea: All humans are innately egocentric and sociocentric. Humans also have (largely undeveloped) rational capacities. Humans begin life as primarily egocentric creatures. Over time, infantile egocentric self-centered thinking merges with sociocentric group-centered thinking. All humans regularly engage in both forms of irrational thought. The extent to which any of us is egocentric or sociocentric is a matter of degree and can change significantly in various situations or contexts. While egocentric and sociocentric propensities are naturally occurring phenomena, rational capacities must be largely developed. It is through the development of rational capacities that we combat irrational tendencies and cultivate critical societies.

Humans Often Distort Reality Through Irrational Lenses

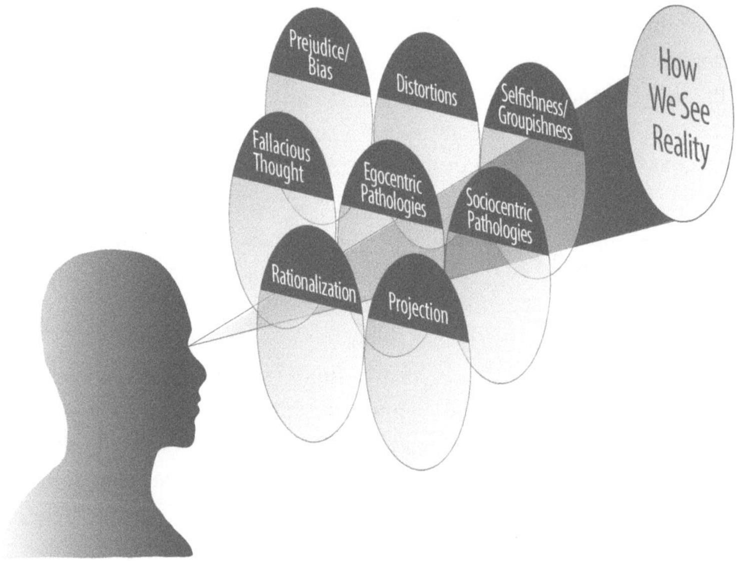

When engaging in irrational pursuits, the mind must decieve itself; it relies on pathologies of thought to do it. The pathologies of thought can be pictured as a set of filters or lenses that:

- cause or "enable" us to see the world according to our perceived interests, without regard to others,
- distort reality so we can get what we want,
- lead us to ignore relevant information to paint a favored picture of the world, based on our vested interests.

These pathologies allow us to decieve ourselves into believing what we want to believe (in order to get what we want or maintain our viewpoint). Pathologies of thought, hence, serve their master—self-deception. They are mainfest in both egocentric and sociocentric thought.

The Problem of Egocentric Thinking

Egocentric thinking comes from the unfortunate fact that humans do not naturally consider the rights and needs of others, nor do we naturally appreciate the point of view of others or the limitations in our own point of view. We become explicitly aware of our egocentric thinking only if trained to do so. We do not naturally recognize our egocentric assumptions, the egocentric way we use information, the egocentric way we interpret data, the source of our egocentric concepts and ideas, the implications of our egocentric thought. We do not naturally recognize our self-serving perspective.

As humans we live with the unrealistic but confident sense that we have fundamentally figured out the way things actually are, and that we have done this objectively. We naturally believe in our intuitive perceptions—however inaccurate. Instead of using intellectual standards in thinking, we often use self-centered psychological standards to determine what to believe and what to reject. Here are the most commonly used psychological standards in human thinking:

"IT'S TRUE BECAUSE I BELIEVE IT." *Innate egocentrism:* I assume that what I believe is true even though I have never questioned the basis for many of my beliefs.

"IT'S TRUE BECAUSE I WANT TO BELIEVE IT." *Innate wish fulfillment:* I believe in, for example, accounts of behavior that put me (or the groups to which I belong) in a positive rather than a negative light even though I have not seriously considered the evidence for the more negative account. I believe what "feels good," what supports my other beliefs, what does not require me to change my thinking in any significant way, what does not require me to admit I have been wrong.

"IT'S TRUE BECAUSE I HAVE ALWAYS BELIEVED IT." *Innate self-validation:* I have a strong desire to maintain beliefs that I have long held, even though I have not seriously considered the extent to which those beliefs are justified, given the evidence.

"IT'S TRUE BECAUSE IT IS IN MY SELFISH INTEREST TO BELIEVE IT." *Innate selfishness:* I hold fast to beliefs that justify my getting more power, money, or personal advantage even though these beliefs are not grounded in sound reasoning or evidence.

Since humans are naturally prone to assess thinking in keeping with the above criteria, it is not surprising that we, as a species, have not developed a significant interest in establishing and teaching legitimate intellectual standards. It is not surprising that our thinking is often flawed.

Feelings That Accompany Egocentrism

These are some of the many feelings that might accompany egocentric thinking. They often occur when egocentric thinking is "unsuccessful." Note that some of these emotions may be concomitant with rational thought — depending on the context and particulars in a given case.

Essential Idea: When egocentric thinking is successful in getting what it wants, positive feelings accompany it. But when egocentric thinking is not able to achieve its purposes, negative feelings result.

The Logic of Egocentrism

Egocentrism has a self-contained logic. To itself, it appears logical. By focusing on its logic we can figure out how it functions. We can figure out its purpose, assumptions, point of view, etc.[1]

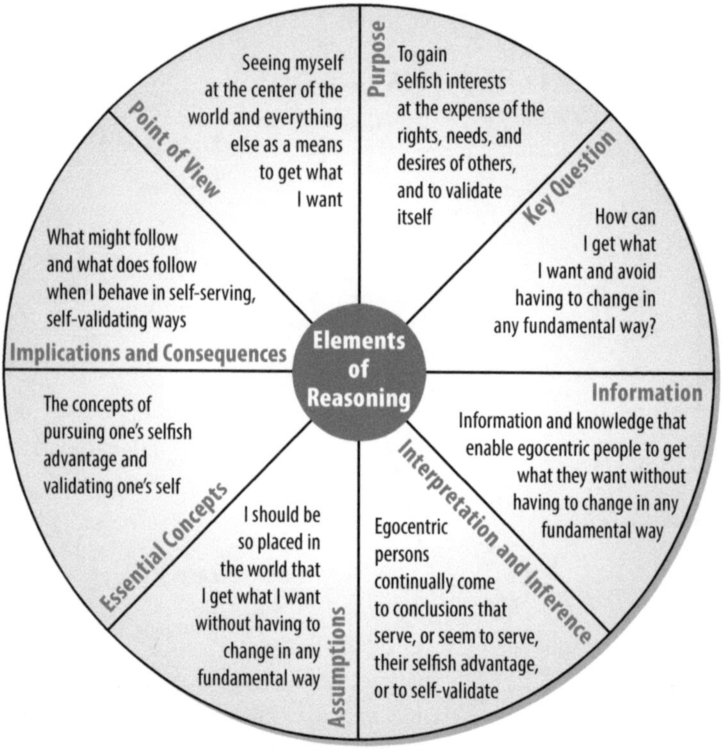

[1] An overview of the elements of reasoning, which provide a structure for understanding this logic and the others in this miniguide, can be found in *The Miniature Guide to Critical Thinking Concepts and Tools*. (see criticalthinking.org)

Distinguishing Egocentric Domination From Egocentric Submission

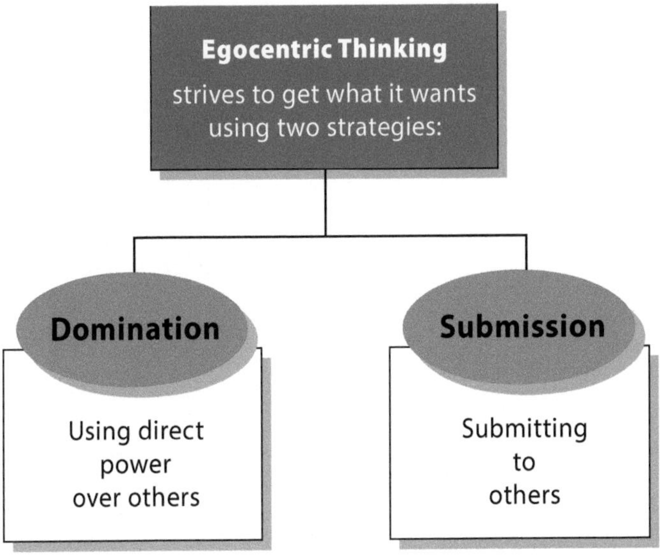

Essential Idea: Two irrational ways to gain and use power are given in two distinct forms of egocentric strategy:

1) The art of dominating others (a direct means to getting what one wants).
2) The art of submitting to others (an indirect means to getting what one wants).

Insofar as we are thinking egocentrically, we seek to satisfy our egocentric desires either directly or indirectly, by exercising power and control over others, or by submitting to those who can act to serve our interest. To put it crudely, egocentric behavior either bullies or grovels. It either threatens those weaker or subordinates itself to those more powerful, or oscillates between them in subtle maneuvers and schemes.

The Logic of Egocentric Domination

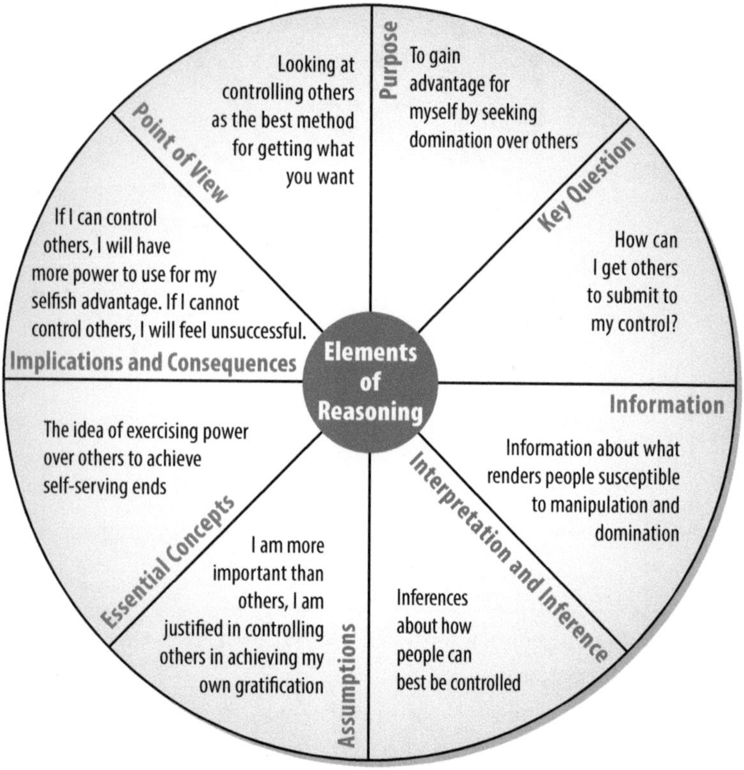

The Logic of Egocentric Submission

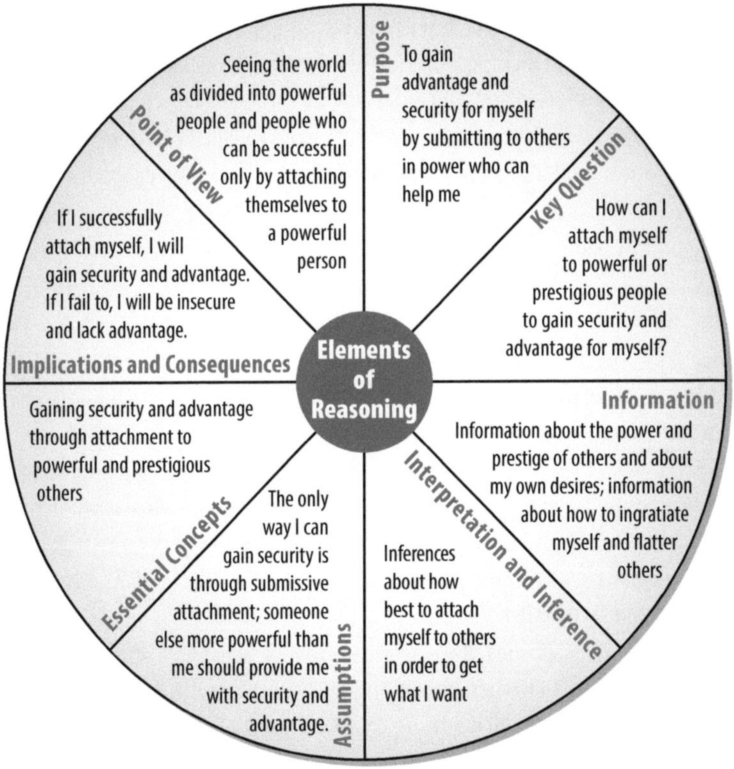

Pathological Dispositions of the Human Mind

An array of interrelated pathological dispositions are inherent in native egocentric thought. To significantly develop as rational persons, we must identify these tendencies in our lives, determining which of them are the most prominent and which the least problematic. As you read them, ask yourself whether you recognize these as processes that occur in your own mind (if you conclude, "not me!" think again):

- egocentric memory: the natural tendency to "forget" evidence and information that do not support our thinking and to "remember" evidence and information that do
- egocentric myopia: the natural tendency to think in an absolutist way within an overly narrow point of view
- egocentric righteousness: the natural tendency to see ourselves in possession of "The Truth"
- egocentric hypocrisy: the natural tendency to ignore flagrant inconsistencies—between what we profess to believe and the actual beliefs our behavior implies, or between the standards we apply to ourselves and those we apply to others
- egocentric oversimplification: the natural tendency to ignore real and important complexities in the world in favor of simplistic notions when consideration of those complexities would require us to modify our beliefs or values
- egocentric blindness: the natural tendency to not notice facts and evidence that contradict our favored beliefs or values
- egocentric immediacy: the natural tendency to over-generalize immediate feelings and experiences, so that when one, or only a few, events in our life seem highly favorable or unfavorable, all of life seems favorable or unfavorable to us
- egocentric absurdity: the natural tendency to fail to notice when our thinking has "absurd" implications

Challenging the Pathological Dispositions of the Human Mind

It is not enough to recognize abstractly that the human mind has a predictable pathology. We must take concrete steps to correct it. This requires us to develop the habit of identifying these tendencies in action. We can all perform these corrections, but only over time and with deliberate practice.

Correcting egocentric memory. We can correct our natural tendency to "forget" evidence and information that do not support our thinking and to "remember" evidence and information that do, by overtly seeking evidence and information that do not support our thinking and directing explicit attention to them. If you try and cannot find such evidence, you should assume you have not conducted your search properly.

Correcting egocentric myopia. We can correct our natural tendency to think in an absolutistic way within an overly narrow point of view by routinely thinking within points of view that conflict with our own. For example, if we are liberal, we can take the time to read books by insightful conservatives. If we are conservative, we can take the time to read books by insightful liberals. If we are North Americans, we can study a contrasting South American point of view or a European or Far-Eastern or Middle-Eastern or African point of view. By the way, if you don't discover significant personal prejudices through this process, you should question whether you are acting in good faith in trying to identify your prejudices.

Correcting egocentric righteousness. We can correct our natural tendency to feel superior in light of our confidence that we possess the truth by regularly reminding ourselves how little we actually know. In this case, we can explicitly state the unanswered questions that surround whatever knowledge we may have. By the way, if you don't discover that there is much more that you do not know than you do, you should question the manner in which you pursued your own ignorance.

Correcting egocentric hypocrisy. We can correct our natural tendency to ignore flagrant inconsistencies between what we profess to believe and the actual beliefs our behavior implies, and inconsistencies between the standards to which we hold ourselves and those to which we hold others. We can do this by regularly comparing the criteria and standards by which we are judging others with those by which we are judging ourselves. If you don't find many flagrant inconsistencies in your own thinking and behavior, you should doubt the accuracy of your search.

Correcting egocentric oversimplification. We can correct our natural tendency to ignore real and important complexities in the world by regularly focusing on those complexities, formulating them explicitly in words, and targeting them. If you don't discover over time that you have oversimplified many important issues, you should question whether you have really confronted the complexities inherent in the issues.

Correcting egocentric blindness. We can correct our natural tendency to ignore facts or evidence that contradict our favored beliefs or values by explicitly seeking out those facts and evidence. If you don't find yourself experiencing significant discomfort as you pursue these facts, you should question whether you are taking them seriously. If you discover that your traditional beliefs were all correct from the beginning, you probably moved to a new and more sophisticated level of self-deception.

Correcting egocentric immediacy. We can correct our natural tendency to over-generalize immediate feelings and experiences by getting into the habit of putting positive and negative events into a larger perspective. You can temper the negative events by reminding yourself of how much you have that many others lack. You can temper the positive events by reminding yourself of how much is yet to be done, of how many problems remain. You know you are keeping an even keel if you find that you have the energy to act effectively in either negative or positive circumstances. You know that you are falling victim to your emotions if and when you are immobilized by them.

Correcting egocentric absurdity. We can correct our natural tendency to ignore thinking that has absurd consequences by making the consequences of our thinking explicit and assessing them for their realism. This requires that we frequently trace the implications of our beliefs and their consequences in our behavior. For example, we should frequently ask ourselves: "If I really believed this, how would I act? Do I really act that way?"

By the way, personal ethics is a fruitful area for disclosing egocentric absurdity. We frequently act in ways that are "absurd"—given what we insist we believe in. If, after what you consider to be a serious search, you find no egocentric absurdity in your life, think again. You are probably self-deceived.

Defense Mechanisms of the Mind

The human mind routinely engages in unconscious processes that are egocentrically motivated, and that strongly influence our behavior. When functioning egocentrically, we seek to get what we want. We see the world from a narrow self-serving perspective. Yet we also see ourselves as driven by purely rational motives. We therefore disguise our egocentric motives as those that appear rational. This disguise necessitates self-deception.

Self-deception is achieved by means of defense mechanisms. The concept of defense mechanisms was first developed by Sigmund and Anna Freud. Defense mechanisms overlap and interrelate with intellectual pathologies as well as with informal fallacies. Here are some of the most common defense mechanisms:

Denial: When a person refuses to believe undisputable evidence or facts in order to maintain a favorable self-image or favored set of beliefs. A basketball player, for example, may deny that there are any real flaws in his game in order to maintain an image of himself as highly skilled at basketball. A "patriot" may deny—in the face of clear-cut evidence—that his country ever violates human rights or acts unjustly.

Identification: When a person takes to himself those qualities and ideals he admires in other people and institutions. Through sociocentric identification he elevates his sense of worth. Examples: a football fan experiencing an inner sense of triumph when his team wins, a parent experiencing a triumph in the success of his children, a citizen feeling elevated by the triumph of his nation's armed forces.

Projection: When a person attributes to another person what he or she feels or thinks in order to avoid unacceptable thoughts and feelings. A wife who doesn't love her husband may accuse him of not loving her (when he really does) in order to unconsciously deal with her dishonesty in the relationship.

Repression: When thoughts, feelings or memories unacceptable to the individual are prevented from reaching consciousness. This often occurs when memories are considered too painful to remember. It can also be a form of "forgetting" because the person doesn't want to remember something unpleasant (such as a dental appointment).

Rationalization: When a person gives reasons (sometimes good reasons) for his behavior, but not the true reasons, because his actions result from unconscious motives he cannot consciously accept. The father who beats his children may rationalize his behavior by saying he is doing it for his children's "own good," so they will become more disciplined, when the true reason is that he has lost control of his behavior.

Stereotyping: When a person lumps people together based on some common characteristic, forming a rigid, biased perception of the group and the individuals in the group. One form of stereotyping comes from cultural bias wherein the person assumes that practices and beliefs in his culture are superior to those in other cultures simply by virtue of being part of his culture. He takes his group to be the measure of all groups and people.

Scapegoating: When a person attempts to avoid criticism of himself by blaming another person, group or thing for his or her own mistakes or faults.

Sublimation: When a person diverts instinctive, primitive or socially unacceptable desires into socially acceptable activities. The sexually unfulfilled drill sergeant may sublimate his sexual energy through aggressive and dominating behavior toward new recruits.

Wishful Thinking: When a person unconsciously misinterprets facts in order to maintain a belief. Wishful thinking leads to false expectations and usually involves seeing things more positively than is reasonable in the situation.

Primary Forms of Sociocentric Thought

Consider four distinct forms of sociocentric thought. These forms function and are manifest in complex relationships with one another; all are destructive.[2] They can be summarized as follows:

1. *Groupishness*[3] *(or group selfishness)*—the tendency on the part of groups to seek the most for the in-group without regard to the rights and needs of others, in order to advance the group's biased interests. Groupishness is almost certainly the primary tendency in sociocentric thinking, the foundational driving force behind it (probably connected to survival in our dim dark past). Everyone in the group is privileged; everyone outside the group is denied group privileges and/or seen as a potential threat.
2. *Group validation*—the tendency on the part of groups to believe their way to be the right way and their views to be the correct views; the tendency to reinforce one another in these beliefs; the inclination to validate the group's views, however dysfunctional or illogical. These may be long-held or newly established views, but in either case, they are perceived by the group to be true and in many cases to advance its interests. This tendency informs the world view from which everyone outside the group is seen and understood and by which everything that happens outside the group is judged. It leads to the problem of *in-group* thinking and behavior—everyone inside the group thinking within a collective logic; everyone outside the group being judged according to the standards and beliefs of the in-group.

---

2 The term sociocentric thought is being reserved for those group beliefs that cause harm or are likely to cause harm. Group thought that is reasonable, useful, or helpful would not fall into this category. In our view, it is important to see sociocentric thought as destructive because otherwise the mind will find a variety of ways to rationalize it. By recognizing it as irrational, we are better able to identify it in our thinking and take command of it.

3 By groupishness we mean group selfishness. This term refers to group pursuit of its interests without sufficient regard for the rights and needs of those outside the group; its counterpart is selfishness, which refers to individual pursuit of one's interests without sufficient regard for the rights and needs of others. We might use the term "group selfishness" for our intended meaning here; but it seems rather to be an oxymoron. How can a group be selfish, given the root word "self," which refers to the individual? The term "groupish" seems a better fit for the purpose. Note that this use of the term "groupish" differs from the way in which evolutionary biologists use the same term. Their use generally refers to the fact that members of a group are aware of their group membership and are aware that there are others (like them) in the group.

3. *Group control*—the tendency on the part of groups to ensure that group members behave in accordance with group expectations. This logic guides the intricate inner workings of the group, largely through enforcement, ostracism, and punishment in connection with group customs, conventions, rules, taboos, mores, and laws. Group control can also take the form of "recruitment" through propaganda and other forms of manipulation. It is often sophisticated and camouflaged.
4. *Group conformity*—a byproduct of the fact that to survive, people must figure out how to fit themselves into the groups they are thrust into or voluntarily choose to join. They must conform to the rules and laws set down by those in control. Dissenters are punished in numerous ways. Group control and group conformity are two sides of the same coin—each presupposes the other.

These four sociocentric tendencies interrelate and overlap in any number of ways and thus should be understood as four parts of an interconnected puzzle.

Sociocentric tendencies largely lie at the unconscious level. It isn't that people are aware of these tendencies and consciously choose to go along with them. Rather, these dispositions are, at least to some extent, hidden by self-deception, rationalization, and other native mechanisms of the mind that keep us from seeing and facing the truth in our thoughts and actions. The mind tells itself one thing on the surface (e.g., we are being fair to all involved) when in fact it is acting upon a different thought entirely (e.g., we are mainly concerned with our own interests). In most instances, the mind can find ways to justify itself—even when engaging in highly unethical acts.[4]

[4] It should be pointed out that there are many circumstances where rational behavior might be confused with sociocentric behavior. For instance, group members may well validate among themselves views that are reasonable. And groups should expect group members to behave in ethical ways. There may also be many other conditions under which it would make sense for an individual to conform to group expectations (e.g. to keep from being tortured or to contribute tc the well being of the planet).

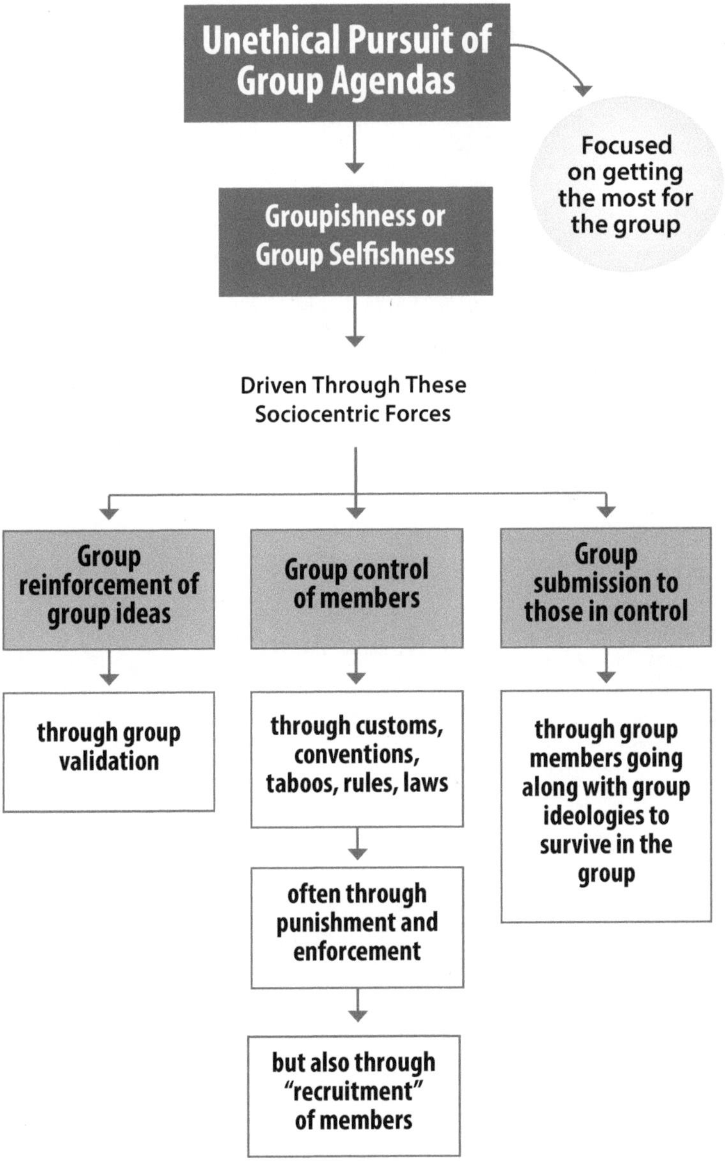

Groupishness, to be effectively "achieved", requires group reinforcement, group control and group submission; this diagram begins to illuminate the complex relationships between and among the four primary forms of sociocentric thought.

Sociocentricity: The Logic of Groupishness

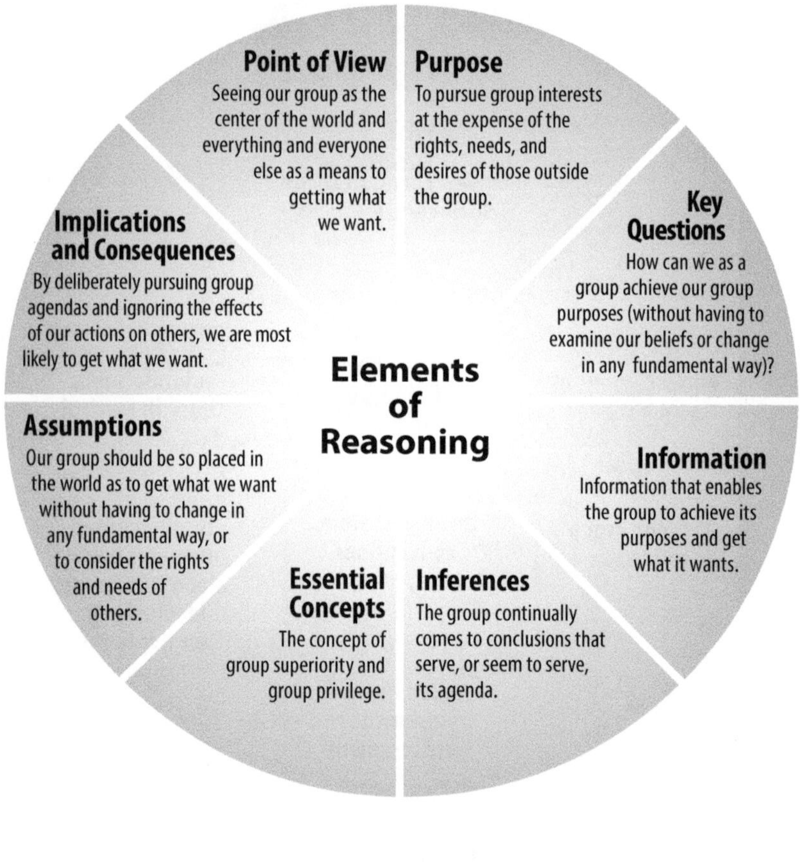

Sociocentricity: The Logic of Group Validation

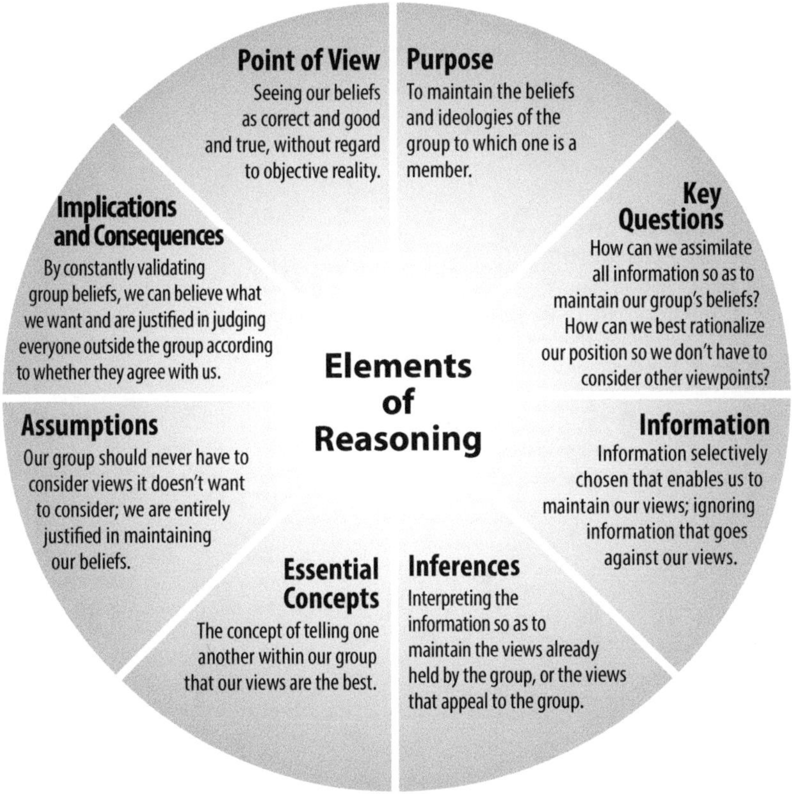

Sociocentricity: The Logic of Group Control

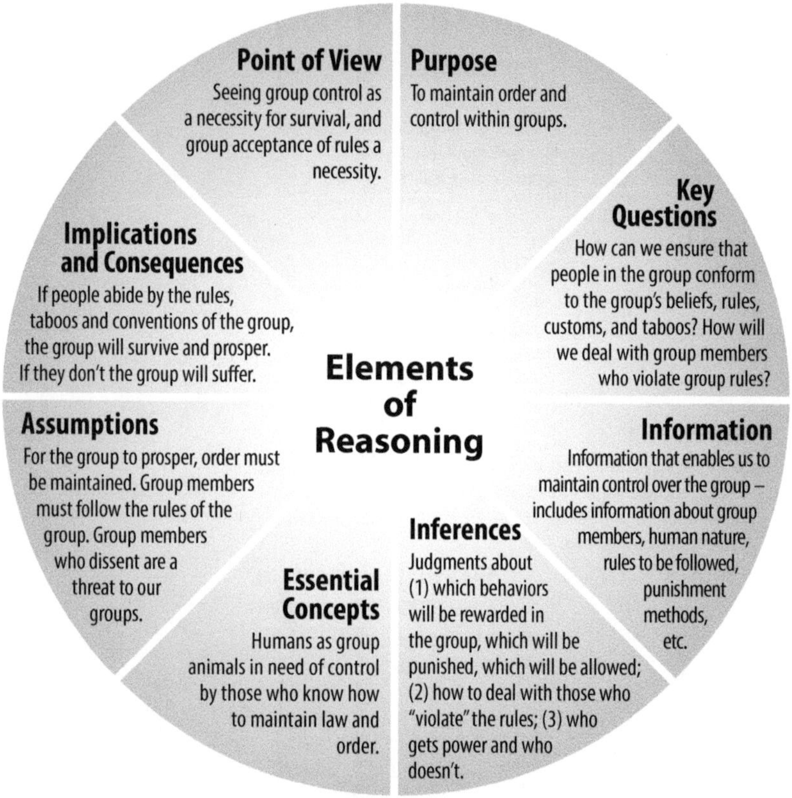

Sociocentricity: The Logic of Conformity

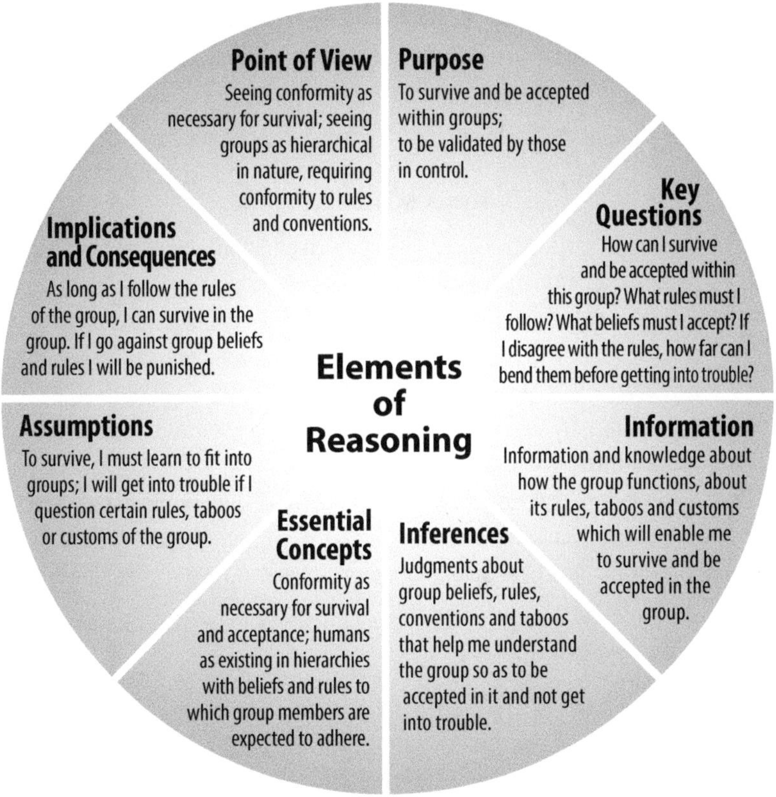

Popular Misunderstandings of the Mind

It is common to believe (erroneously) that:

- Emotion and reason often conflict with each other.
- Emotion and reason function independently of each other.
- It is possible to be an emotional person and hence do little reasoning.
- It is possible to be a rational person and hence experience little emotion.
- Rational persons are cold and mechanical, like Mr. Spock.
- Emotional persons are lively, energetic, warm, but poor reasoners.

In These Mistaken Views:

1. One must give up the possibility of a rich emotional life if one decides to become a rational person.
2. One must give up rationality if one is to live a passionate life.

These Misunderstandings:

- Lead us to think of thought and emotion as if they were oil and water rather than inseparable functions of mind.
- Lead us away from realizing the thinking underlying our emotions and the emotions that influence our thinking.
- Lead us to think that there is nothing we can do to control our emotional life.

Emotional Intelligence and Critical Thinking

Emotion: A state of consciousness having to do with the arousal of feelings. Refers to any of the personal reactions, pleasant or unpleasant, that one may have in a situation.

Intelligence: The ability to learn or understand from experience or to respond successfully to new experiences, the ability to acquire and retain knowledge. Implies the use of reason in solving problems and directing conduct effectively.

Emotional Intelligence: Bringing intelligence to bear upon emotions. Guiding emotions through high quality reason. Implies that high quality reasoning in a situation will lead to more satisfactory emotional states than low quality reasoning.

Critical Thinking provides the link between:

Intelligence ⟷ Emotion

Critical Thinking:

- brings intelligence to bear upon our emotional life
- enables us to take command of our emotions
- enables us to make good judgments
- provides us with a satisfactory emotional life

Essential Idea: When our thinking is of high quality, rational emotions follow. When we develop rational emotions, we think reasonably.

Some Basic Definitions

Affect: The dimension of the mind comprised of emotions and desires. Affect is the counterpart to cognition.

Cognition: The dimension of the mind that thinks. Through cognition we make sense of the world. We figure things out. We make assumptions, inferences and judgments. We interpret situations and experiences. We conceptualize, we formulate ideas. Cognition is the counterpart to affect.

Critical Thinking: A disciplined, self-directed cognitive process leading to high quality decisions and judgments through the analysis, assessment and reformulation of thinking. It presupposes understanding of the parts of thinking, or elements of reasoning, as well as the intellectual standards by which reasoning is assessed and intellectual traits which dispose us to think in deep and honest ways.

Defense Mechanism: A self-deceptive process used by the mind to avoid dealing with unpleasant realities such as accepting responsibility for one's actions, or giving up a selfish desire while deceiving oneself into thinking one's behavior is rational and one's thinking justifiable. Through the use of defense mechanisms the mind can avoid conscious recognition of negative feelings such as guilt, pain, anxiety, etc.

Egocentrism: Any mental state derived from self-deception and leading to irrational behavior and/or emotions. It involves thinking that systematically excludes, ignores or violates the rights and needs of others or keeps one trapped in a dysfunctional self-destructive frame of mind. Egocentrism is the native condition of the undeveloped, uncultivated mind.

Egocentric Domination: The egocentric tendency of the mind to seek what it wants through the irrational use of direct power over, or intimidation of, people. Egocentric domination, or "top dog" behavior may be overt or covert. On the one hand, dominating egocentrism can involve harsh, dictatorial, tyrannical, or bullying behavior (e.g., a physically abusive spouse). On the other hand, it might involve subtle messages and behavior that imply the use of control or force if "necessary" (e.g., a supervisor reminding a subordinate, by quiet innuendo, that his or her employment is contingent upon unquestioning obedience).

Egocentric Submission: The egocentric tendency of the mind to join and serve people it deems as more powerful as a means of getting what it wants. Egocentric submission is the opposite of egocentric domination. Using this form of "underdog thinking," the person joins and serves more powerful others, who then: (1) give one a sense of personal importance, (2) protect one, and (3) share with one some of the benefits of their success. The irrational person uses both egocentric domination and submission, though not to the same extent. Those who seem to be more successful in submitting to more powerful others tend to do so. Those who seem to be more successful in using overt force and control tend to dominate. Submissive behavior can be seen publicly in the relationship of rock stars or sport stars to their admiring followers. Most social groups have an internal "pecking order," with some playing roles of leader and most playing roles of followers. A fairminded rational person seeks neither to dominate nor to irrationally submit to others.

Egocentric Immediacy: The irrational tendency noted by Piaget wherein a person over-generalizes from a set of positive or negative events to either a "Isn't life wonderful" or "Isn't life awful" state of mind. Instead of accurately interpreting situations, the mind over-generalizes, seeing the world either in sweeping negative or positive terms.

Emotional Intelligence: Bringing intelligence to bear upon emotions. Guiding emotions through high quality reason. Implies that high quality reasoning in a situation will lead to more satisfactory emotional states than low quality reasoning.

Human Mind: The processes created by the brain comprised of cognition and affect, more particularly: thinking, feeling and wanting. These processes can be conscious or unconscious.

Irrationality: The mind's use of evidence and reasoning in the attempt either to gain unjustified advantage over others, or to maintain an unjustified self image, or to hide a dysfunctional mental state or posture. Pathological Dispositions: Innate tendencies of the human mind created by native egocentrism and leading to systematic distortion of reality. The pathological dispositions of mind often result in unethical, harmful thoughts and behavior. These dispositions are the opposite of intellectual dispositions such as intellectual integrity, intellectual humility, intellectual perseverance, intellectual courage, intellectual autonomy, and intellectual sense of justice.

Rationality: The mind's appropriate use of evidence and reasoning in the attempt to see things objectively and act in accordance with what is reasonable in the situation.

Self-Deception: The natural human tendency to deceive oneself about one's true motivations, character, or identity. This phenomenon is so common to humans that the human species might well be defined "the self-deceiving animal." Through self-deception, humans are able to ignore unpleasant realities and problems in their thinking and behavior. Self-deception reinforces self-righteousness and intellectual arrogance. It enables us to pursue selfish interests while disguising our motives as altruistic or reasonable. Through self-deception, humans have "justified," and continue to justify, flagrantly unethical acts, policies, and practices. All humans engage in self-deception—but not to the same degree.

Sociocentrism: An extension of egocentric identity from the self ("I am superior") to the group ("We are superior"). It occurs naturally in the human mind and is based on the assumption that one's own social group is inherently and self-evidently superior to all others (since "we" belong to it). When members of a group or society see their group as superior, and so consider the group's views as self-evidently correct and their actions self-evidently justified, they have a tendency to project this superiority into all of their thinking and, thus, to think closed-mindedly and simplistically. Dissent and doubt are then considered disloyal and irresponsible. Those who question the group are made the object of suspicion or scorn. There is no society known to the authors that does not foster sociocentrism under the guise of patriotism.

The Thinker's Guide Library

Rowman & Littlefield is the proud distributor of the Thinker's Guide Library developed by the Foundation for Critical Thinking. Please visit www.rowman.com or call 1-800-462-640 for more information. Bulk order discounts available.

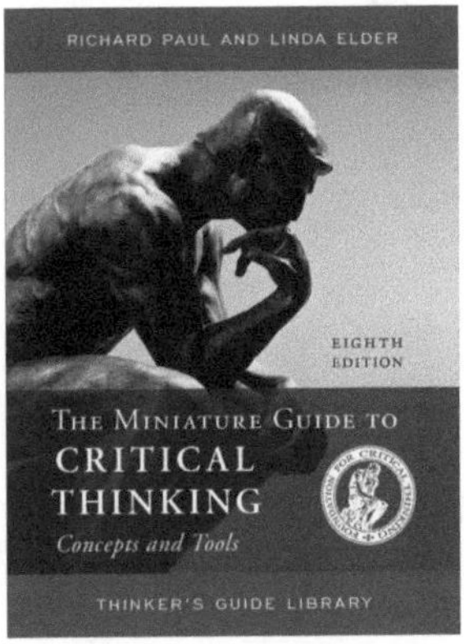

For Everyone

The Miniature Guide to Critical Thinking Concepts & Tools, Eighth Edition
Paperback 9781538134948
eBook 9781538134955

The Thinker's Guide to Ethical Reasoning
Paperback 9780944583173
eBook 9781538133781

The Thinker's Guide to Fallacies
Paperback 9780944583272
eBook 9781538133774

The Art of Asking Essential Questions
Paperback 9780944583166
eBook 9781538133804

Fact Over Fake: A Critical Thinker's Guide to Media Bias and Political Propaganda
Paperback 9781538143940
Hardback 9781538143933
eBook 9781538143957

The Thinker's Guide to Engineering Reasoning
Paperback 9780944583333
eBook 9781538133798

The Thinker's Guide to Analytic Thinking
Paperback 9780944583197
eBook 9781538133750

The Thinker's Guide to Socratic Questioning
Paperback 9780944583319
eBook 9781538133842

The Nature and Functions of Critical & Creative Thinking
Paperback 9780944583265
eBook 9781538133958

Thinker's Guide to the Human Mind
Paperback 9780944583586
eBook 9781538133880

The Thinker's Guide to Scientific Thinking
Paperback 9780985754426
eBook 9781538133811

The Thinker's Guide to Clinical Reasoning
Paperback 9780944583425
eBook 9781538133873

For Students

The Aspiring Thinker's Guide to Critical Thinking
Paperback 9780944583418
eBook 9781538133767

The Thinker's Guide for Students on How to Study & Learn a Discipline, Second Edition
Paperback 9781632340009
eBook 9781538133835

The International Critical Thinking Reading and Writing Test, Second Edition
Paperback 9780944583326
eBook 9781538133965

The Student Guide to Historical Thinking
Paperback 9780944583463
eBook 9781538133941

How to Read a Paragraph, second edition
Paperback 9780944583494
eBook 9781538133828

How to Write a Paragraph
Paperback 9780944583227
eBook 9781538133866

For Educators

The Miniature Guide to Practical Ways for Promoting Active and Cooperative Learning, Third Edition
Paperback 9780944583135
eBook 9781538133903

A Critical Thinker's Guide to Educational Fads
Paperback 9780944583340
eBook 9781538133910

A Guide for Educators to Critical Thinking Competency Standards
Paperback 9780944583302
eBook 9781538133934

How to Improve Student Learning: 30 Practical Ideas
Paperback 9780944583555
eBook 9781538133859

The Thinker's Guide to Intellectual Standards
Paperback 9780944583395
eBook 9781538133927